A Treasury of GERMAN Trademarks

BDG

The sign of the Bund Deutscher Gebrauchgraphiker (Alliance of German Graphic Artists) designed by Karl Schulpig circa 1924.

A Treasury Of GERMAN Trademarks

VOLUME ONE

1850-1925

COMPILATION AND BOOK DESIGN BY

LESLIE CABARGA

FOREWORD BY STEVE HELLER

FIRST EDITION JANUARY 1982

LIBRARY OF CONGRESS CATALOG CARD NUMBER: 81-71799
INTERNATIONAL STANDARD BOOK NUMBER: 0-910158-89-4

Printed in the United States of America.

ART DIRECTION BOOK COMPANY

10 East 39th Street
New York, N.Y. 10016
(212) 889-6500

BITTE SCHWARZ UND WEISS ABZUG DIESEM BLATTE BEIZU
J. F. Lehmann's Verlag
München
Paul Heysestraße 26
Organisation
sen-Nummer
Deutschland
8. Typograph
Leitung
9. Orga
eklame-Agentur
raveur
ithograph
apier-Fabrikant
rucker
Privat-Druckerei
Verleger oder Bu
GENAUE ANGABEN BEZUEGLICH SC
Erdacht
Gezeichnet
Datum, wenn
5 cm.
R
DEU
DEUTS
1894 GE
GRAP
Vereinigt mit dem 1834 begründeten Journal für Buchdruckerkunst, Schriftgießerei und verwandte Fächer
FR. RICHTER GMBH.
BUCH- UND KUNSTDRUCKEREI • BUCHBINDEREI
D./V.
Fa.
Clarence Pearson Hornung,
N e w Y o r k C i t y
Desings at 48 West 48th Street.
Betr. Ihren Bri

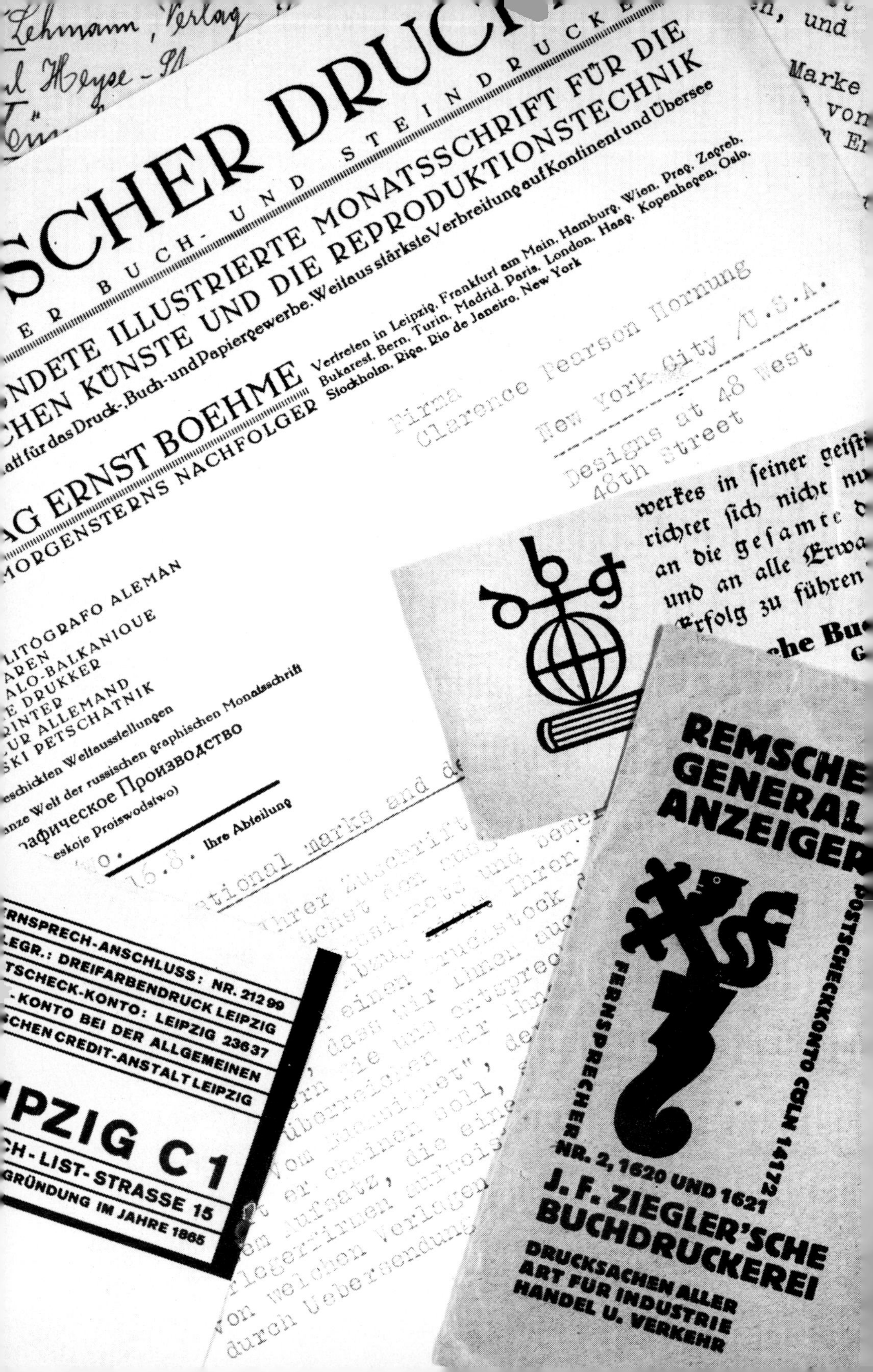

SCHER DRUCK
BUCH- UND STEINDRUCK
NDETE ILLUSTRIERTE MONATSSCHRIFT FÜR DIE
CHEN KÜNSTE UND DIE REPRODUKTIONSTECHNIK
att für das Druck-, Buch- und Papiergewerbe. Weitaus stärkste Verbreitung auf Kontinent und Übersee
AG ERNST BOEHME
MORGENSTERNS NACHFOLGER
Vertreten in Leipzig, Frankfurt am Main, Hamburg, Wien, Prag, Zagreb, Bukarest, Bern, Turin, Madrid, Paris, London, Haag, Kopenhagen, Oslo, Stockholm, Riga, Rio de Janeiro, New York
LITÓGRAFO ALEMAN
ALO-BALKANIQUE
E DRUKKER
UR ALLEMAND
SKI PETSCHATNIK
Ihre Abteilung
Firma
Clarence Pearson Hornung
New York City / U.S.A.
Designs at 48 West
48th Street
werkes in seiner geist
richtet sich nicht nu
an die gesamte
und an alle Erwa
Erfolg zu führen
REMSCHE
GENERAL
ANZEIGER
POSTSCHECKKONTO CÖLN 14172
FERNSPRECHER NR. 2, 1620 UND 1621
J. F. ZIEGLER'SCHE
BUCHDRUCKEREI
DRUCKSACHEN ALLER
ART FÜR INDUSTRIE
HANDEL U. VERKEHR
ERNSPRECH-ANSCHLUSS: NR. 21299
LEGR.: DREIFARBENDRUCK LEIPZIG
TSCHECK-KONTO: LEIPZIG 23637
-KONTO BEI DER ALLGEMEINEN
SCHEN CREDIT-ANSTALT LEIPZIG
IPZIG C1
CH-LIST-STRASSE 15
GRÜNDUNG IM JAHRE 1865

Dedication

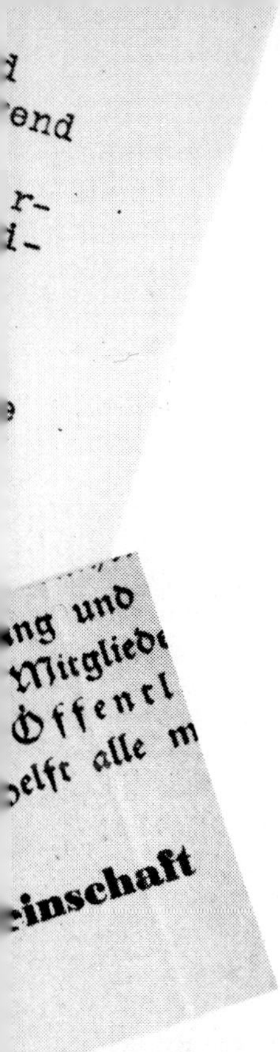

To Clarence Pearson Hornung, graphic artist par excellence and friend. It is no cliche to say that without him this book could never have been accomplished.

In 1928 Clarence began correspondence with prominent firms and designers in Germany to collect trademarks for a book called "International Marks and Devices of the Printing Industry". He was soon inundated with material from the German designers who presumably sought exposure in the American market. When the original publisher backed out, Clarence moved on to other projects and the German trademarks were put aside until 1980 when I acquired the collection from him.

As an illustrator, Clarence Hornung's decorative border work for advertising enhanced the pages of many major publications in the 20's and 30's and frequently appeared in the Art Director's Annuals. He became a trademark specialist and claims 500 designs for private industry and the U.S. Government to his credit. He has written almost 30 books on various aspects of lettering, art and design. Now at 82, Clarence is still active with more projects in the works than many a younger man could keep track of.

Foreword

By Steve Heller

Before you is a treasure trove of visual symbols, imprints and logos — trademarks galore created during the early years of the twentieth century. Many images herein are so delightfully nouveau that they look as though they were designed only yesterday. The Germans, whom we must thank for these visual delights, spawned virtuoso graphic artists for five centuries — from Albrecht Durer to Georg Grosz. Not only were they acerbic social commentators presenting significant, emotion-charged themes through powerful often times grotesque, woodcuts and engravings, German artists in general were also inventive designers, applying a finely tuned compositional sense to both narrative art and functional graphics. Whereas Paris was the fin de siecle capital of modern painting, Berlin, Munich, Weimar and Dessau (the latter being the homes of the Bauhaus) were hotbeds of modern design. German applied art is an amalgam of exemplary craft and extraordinary imagination, wherein classical and avant-garde modes are clearly visible. The keen ability to elicit response on various psychological levels in the manner of the Expressionists is apparent in many of the symbols reproduced here. It is the clever marriage of various art forms in the service of commerce which makes these particular trademarks so fascinating. It is the influence exerted by the graphic symbol on everyday life that makes this field of study so compelling.

Although the dictionary defines trademarks as a commercial tool, the graphic symbol clearly functions in non-commercial arenas. The well designed symbol is decidedly a key to the subconcious, evoking both positive and negative responses. Freud and Jung among others have waxed eloquently on the significance of symbols and the psyche. Symbols can intensify particular passions or pacify the mind. Using the most catholic of definitions it is safe to say that the crucifix is the most successful and universal "trademark" in existence. It is both immediately recognizable and accessible, and its reproduction is possible given any medium. Its economy is unchallenged, yet the cross can be embellished with ornaments and not lose its power. It conjures a multitude of perceptions: Originally a symbol of oppression and pain, its meaning was redefined by those who were oppressed. Historically, it was a rallying point for those who believed, but it also served as an instrument to instill fear in those who did not. Who can forget the countless book illustrations in which Richard the Lionhearted and his minions carried the cross, emblazoned on their breastplates and banners, off to the Crusades? And let us not forget Count Dracula's reaction to the cross before his eyes — such a response would warm the blood of any logo designer.

A well designed visual symbol demands immediate attention. A trademark is a mode of graphic shorthand which more than any other device condenses and simplifies complex notions into a concrete form. It is a sign-language that substitutes for one word or an entire sentence — modern day Sanskrit. It has myriad functions, among them the identification with or protest against a particular cause or issue. Radically different responses by different viewers to the same image are often intended. For example, the Swastika was originally revered throughout the ancient world as a symbol of good luck and a happy life. Its most recent applicants created a "trademark" which inspired Nazi followers, terrified those they oppressed and enraged their enemies. It quickly became the most despised logo of the twentieth century. Often symbols are perceived differently because of the tenor of the times: the "Rising Sun," the Japanese national emblem, admired today for its beautiful simplicity (characteristic of all Japanese design) was, during World War II, a distinct symbol of treachery and deception. The "Nuclear Disarmament" (ND) symbol, once perceived to be the logo of "chicken littles," was transformed by events into the rallying point for an entire generation. Quite clearly, these examples evidence the power instilled in, and the "magic" inherent in, well proportioned graphic symbols. These images are only the tip of the iceberg, a part of an enormous legacy.

In colloquial terms, "trademarks" are used to signify abstracts such as ideology, philosophy and theology (as described above). However, the dictionary offers a more parochial definition which is limited to their commercial function (represented by the majority of the images in this book). These trademarks are decendants of the merchant's mark — a brand, of sorts, initiated during the fourteenth century, employed by merchants and manufacturers to inform the illiterate population as to who owns what. Teamsters, for example, would know where to deliver merchandise because the mark would be prominently placed on its covering. Often philanthropists would hang a printed version of their marks on church windows to show their largesse— donations of food, guns, or building materials would be represented within the image. These marks, prevalent from the 1300s to the 1600s, were composed of heraldic imagery (such as regal animals, swords and shields) and varied combinations of simple geometric forms (similar to the brands of the ranch owners of the American west). During the seventeenth century large outdoor trade signs were the rage, employing more literal symbols. For instance, the rebus was common — a sign with the name of a merchant such as "Churchill" would show a picture of a church and a hill tied together through some design motif. Other signs would have simple stylized representations of the specific trade—eye glasses for an eye doctor, anvil for a blacksmith, etc. Until the Jugenstil movement revolutionized design in Germany, images borrowed from antiquity were the most commonplace German logos. Use of the new, organic curvilinear style opened the door to abstraction. Most of the "modern" trademarks in this volume are based on geometric shapes. The circle was the foremost basis of design; then the line and band, triangle, square, diamond, pentagon, hexagon, octagon and star. Pictograms were prolifically used and often were streamlined versions of the classical imagery. The flat colors of Jugenstil and the blackness of Expressionist graphics were masterfully adapted. Further, the designers seemed to have a great deal of fun. Illustrators and poster designers, such as Emil Preetorius or Thomas Theodore Heine, included cartoon elements in their design (much in the manner of the French originated "Michelin Tire Man"). Others seem to have enjoyed the stream of consciousness manipulations derived from the puzzle-like search for the perfect solution. All in all this was a grand time for trademark designers.

Unlike Switzerland, a nation reflected by its clean, stolid predictable design, Germany is a nation of contradictions. The same people who developed revolutionary forms of expression also produced its antithesis. Yet, one marvels at the facility evidenced in this book, and at all German book, poster and magazine design during the first three decades of this century.

Introduction

By Leslie Cabarga

American designers have long looked with awe at the German graphic arts. In the early teens artists such as Ludwig Hohlwein and Lucian Bernhard shocked poster designers out of their Victorian malaise with bold designs utilizing simple shapes and flat backgrounds. In the 1930's the German poster and graphic art magazine, "Gebrauchsgraphik" was avidly collected by American designers looking for fresh ideas. The work of German and other European artists such as Joseph Binder and A.M. Cassandre began to typify for Americans the streamlined look of modern art deco graphics. Art directors today still refer to well-worn copies of the German magazine "Twen" (which ended publication in the 1970's) for inspiration and the bold, clean approach which has come to be known as the "Swiss" school of designing.

It is interesting to compare the designs in this book with those being done in America at the same period. The German marks are more restrained, more concerned with pure design and symbolism within a given form. American marks consisted of the company name distinctively hand lettered or comic and human characters such as The Old Dutch Maid, Aunt Jemima, Rastus the Cream of Wheat man, and Mr. Peanut. On the other hand, compare F.H. Ehmcke's 1911 design for the Free Association for the Introduction of the Fine Arts with the Chase Manhattan Bank trademark designed by Tom Geismar in 1960. Many of the marks in this book might have been designed today; despite their 50 years of age, they still look fresh and timeless.

It would, however, be innacurate to say that this collection is entirely typical of all trademarks produced in Germany at the time. In most cases these marks are by the better known designers and for the better class of firm which both appreciated and could afford to hire them. German Industry ascribed a greater value to the trademark than the Americans at the same period. Often the trademark was the only visual element in packaging and advertising. Consequently, there developed many trademark specialists, a condition that was not to occur in America for many years. Also unique in Germany was the frequent publication of high quality, limited edition monographs of an artist's work.

In the preface to one such monograph in 1929, the designer Konrad Jochheim gave his interpretation of the trademark's beginnings in Germany. He theorized that the word "wappen" (coat of arms or heraldic symbol) might have

F.H. Ehmcke, 1911

Tom Geismar, 1960

been derived from the work "wappnen": to arm. The German father of Medieval days would engrave his mark onto spears and shields for his sons to inherit. From identifying marks such as these heraldic symbols evolved. And perhaps due to the fact that the Europeans are surrounded by their ancient history (as opposed to relatively modern America), the German designers worked with the heraldic traditions closely in mind. This accounts for the frequent use of such classic symbols in their designs as the lightning bolt, cross, arrow and animals such as the eagle, stallion and the mythological griffon.

Jochheim goes on to liken modern trademark designers to the Herald of past ages who created the symbols and kept records of them. He described modern trademarks as the "weapons and armor" in today's battle for recognition in the marketplace. The package emblazoned with the trademark is the armor of the product protecting it from imitation and competition (the German word, "shutz-marke," which is their equivalent to "trademark," means "protection mark"). "And," continued Jochheim, "that's why beauty of form is important since beauty is always victorious."

Fritz Hellmut Ehmcke, whose work is featured prominently in this book, was one of Germany's foremost designers. Besides a prodigious output of trademarks his work included architecture, interior design, posters, illustration and type design. Many German designers are found to be similarly versatile. Ehmcke even designed his own word for his trademarks: "kennbilder" translates approximately to mean a picture instantly recognizable; a simple design which tells the story at one glance and evokes an emotional response in the viewer. This was the goal Ehmcke set for the work he designed. When Ehmcke began creating trademarks in 1902, his simple approach to design was a response to the "confusing" ornament of Art Nouveau.

Wilhelm Deffke and Carl Ernst Hinkefuss formed the nucleus of an important design studio known as "Wilhelmwerk." They joined forces in 1907 to "propagate the old German craftsmanship." "Wilhelmwerk is the key word for our workshop in German craftsmanship. A quality sign for our creations, it also shows the specialty of an art based on decades old grounds with psychological advertising powers."

Wilhelmwerk was apparently responsible for applying the swastika to the service of the German Reich. This age old symbol, the swastika or hooked cross, was considered a mystic healing sign before being usurped forever by the Germans and losing it's value as a popular design element. One wonders how many mosaic tile floors utilizing the swastika as part of the decorative border must have been ripped up in America during the 1940's.

In addition to commercial designs (for which only the higher class of advertiser was serviced), Wilhelmwerk did many Government commissions such as the German Gymnastic Association and others based on classic symbols. Wilhelmwerk did much to further the strong simple "black" style of German trademark design.

The work of Karl Schulpig is some of the most ingenious by the German designers. His services were much sought after in other countries as well and his success spawned a host of imitators. Schulpig's ability to create a picture representing the firm's product while incorporating the firm's initials was his most outstanding feature. Yet not all of his ingenuity is immediately apparent in viewing his works. It is sometimes necessary to look past the stylized picturizations of the firm's purpose to discover the monogram contained within or created by the picture. Schulpig's approach to trademark conceptualization is helpful to designers today, too many of whose work achieves the bold visual appearance while failing to carry with it the underlying substance of meaning and purpose. While Schulpig favored heavy black masses, the element of humor running through his work served to mitigate the otherwise ominous character of such design. Oddly, though men like Schulpig, Jochheim and Ehmcke made use of straight lines and sharp angles, there was not a great concern with technical accuracy in the final rendering. This I discovered while retouching the designs, which was necessary in some cases because of extreme enlargement. Emphasizing concept over flawless execution lent a "hand made" appearance and a greater warmth to their designs. The "artistic" look was quite acceptable even in the most high-class advertising of the period extending into the 1930's (in America as well as Germany.)

Rudolph Koch, known for his calligraphy and type design, is represented by two examples of his work (see 1921). While these designs may seem more like monograms than trademarks, they are typical of the German approach to much of this work. Immersed as they were in "black letter script" or "old English" text and headline type faces, the calligraphic trademark was quite common and can be seen throughout this book.

Walter Kersting was another of Germany's prominent advertising and trademark designers. In a beautifully printed self-promotional booklet published in 1925, Kersting listed the price for all rights to a trademark design as being between 1 and 5000 Reichmarks. He urged clients to go for the higher price and the better quality trademark because in the long run it was cheaper. "One of the meanest tasks is the bettering of a mediocre trademark".

It is unfortunate that information is not available on artists such as Hermann Virl, Max Korner, Paul Renner and Karl Prinz, all prominent designers represented in this book.

In the 1929 monograph previously quoted Konrad Jochheim gave his rules for a successful trademark, rules that seem as applicable today as when they were written:

"1. Impressiveness; An impressive trademark is achieved by explaining the quality of the product. 2. Simplicity; A mark must be simple because of the necessity to reproduce it at all sizes and in any medium. 3. Originality; The mark must not be confused with any other. 4. Timelessness; The mark must not evolve out of a fashionable mood. 5. The right mark is the fundamental advertising tool of the company."

Eigenmarken

**Personal Marks of some of Germany's foremost trademark designers of the past.*

Opposite page: Hans Beyer-Preusser and Fritz Glaseman; Fritz Hellmut Ehmcke; O.W. Hadank, Max Körner

Below: Konrad Jochheim, Walter Maria Kersting; Karl Schulpig; Karl Schulpig

1865-1908

F. Bruckmann Co. (publisher), Development of logos
(ca. 1865) Unknown artist
(1900) Thomas Von Rysselberghe
(1905) Fritz Hellmut Ehmcke (Steglitzer Workshop)
(1908) Walter Tiemann

F. Bruckmann Co.
(ca. 1860) Unknown artist

1875

F. Bruckmann Co.
C. Kargey

F. Bruckmann Co.
(1910) Walter Tiemann
(1910) Walter Tiemann
(1912) Paul Renner
(1912) Karl Hönig

1915

F. Bruckmann Co.
Paul Renner

(1880) Unknown artist (two marks), *Franz Hanfstaengl Co.*(printer?)
(1887) Prof. Otto Hupp, *R. Oldenbourg Co.* (book publisher)
(1912) Unknown artist, *R. Oldenbourg Co.*

1850

J.G. Schelter and Giesecke (Insurance?)
Unknown Artists

1850

1899-1910

(1899) Prof. Peter Behrens, *Insel Verlag* (publisher)
(1907) Eric Gill (British), *Insel Verlag*
(1899) Beckmann, *H. Schmincke and Co.* (fine artists' paints)
(1910) F. H. Ehmcke, *H. Schmincke and Co.*

(1902) F.H.E., *Allgemeine Berline* (automobile sales)
(1904) F.H.E., *Brauerei Zum Grünen Baum* (brewery)
(1904) Wilhelm Ehringhausen, *J.F. Lehmann Verlag* (publisher)

1904-1914

(1904) Thomas Theodor Heine, *Albert Langen Verlag* (Publisher)
(1914) F.H.E., *Albert Langen Verlag*
(1905) Hans Beyer-Preusser and Fritz Glasemann, *Frauenheim Expedition* (Women's Mission)
(1905) E.R.Weiss, *Julius Bard Verlag* (publisher)

(1905) F.H.E., *Franz Hager Co.* (perfume)
E.R.Weiss, *The National Gallery* (Germany)
Hans Beyer-Preusser and Fritz Glasemann, *Julius Bruckner Co.* (printer—stone lithography)
F.H.E., *Klinkhardt and Eyssen* (photographic Studio)

1908

F.H.E., *Ludwig Hoell* (engraver)
F.H.E., *Heintze and Blanckertz Co.* (steel pens)
F.H.E., *Wilhelm Kluckow* (tailor)
F.H.E., *M. Schieferdecker* (cigar store)

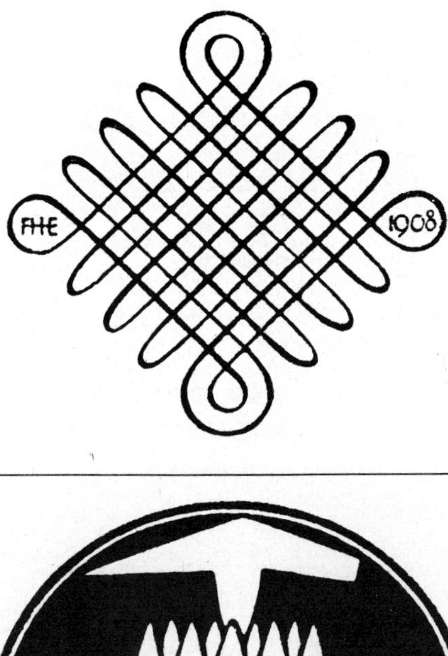

1908

F.H.E., *Rheinische Linoleumwerke* (wall and floor coverings)

1909-1925

K. und B. Verlag (publisher)
(1909) E.R. Weiss
(1922) Wilhelm Punneshe
(1924) Prof. Emil Preetorius
(1925) Prof. Emil Preetorius

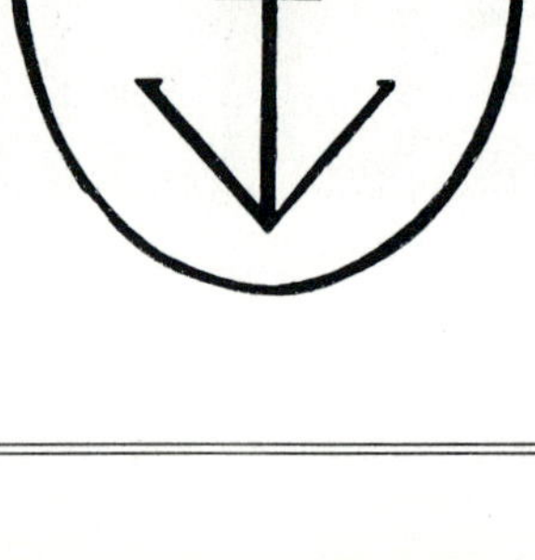

1925

K. und B. Verlag
Prof. Emil Preetorius

1909-1910

F.H.E., *Benz Inc.* (automobiles)
F.H.E., *Dr. Erwin Quedenfeld* (photographer)
F.H.E., *Karl Brunner'sche Buchhandlung* (bookstore)

Prof. A. Niemann, *Dietrich Reimer/Ernst Vohren* (publisher)
Walter Tiemann, Unknown company (art publisher)

1911

F.H.E., *Workshop for Calligraphy*

F.H.E., *Home Improvement League* (Dusseldorf)

Zero (Hans Schleger), Unknown Company

F.H.E., *Free Association - for Introduction of the Fine Arts*

1912

F.H.E., for book: *"Judenpflege," Eugen Diederichs Verlag* (publisher)

1912

Unknown artist, *Richard Hermes Verlag* (publisher)
F.H.E., *Berndorfer Metallwarenfabrik* (metal ware)
F.H.E., *Prof. G. Metzendorf* (architect)

Walter Tiemann, *Kurt Wolff Verlag* (publisher)
(1923) Lucian Bernhard
(1925) Emil Preetorius

1913-1914

Unknown artist, *Rupprecht Presse* (printer)
F.H.E., *Parfumerie Scherk* (perfume)
F.H.E., *Rupprecht Presse* (printer)

1914

Konrad Jochheim, *A. Wilzbacher Möbel Fabrik* (furniture)

1915

August Wiesener, *Textile Design Tradeshow in Hamburg*

1915

Prof. Georg Friedrich and Ernst Pickardt, *Wohlegemuth and Lissner Verleger* (publishers)

1915

Konrad Jochheim, *Werner Dohany Verlag* (publisher)
F.H.E., *Gesellschaft zur Förderung Deutscher Kunst des 20 Jahrhunderts (Society for promotion of German art in the 20th century)*

1915

Ernst Pickardt, Unknown company

1916

F.H.E., "*Die Hochschule*" (magazine: The Highschool)
Wilhelmwerk (Carl Ernst Hinkefuss and Wilhelm H. Deffke), *Manoli Co.* (cigarettes)
F.H.E., *Carl Mannesmann* (steel)

1917

Wilhelmwerk, *Original Mark of the Aryan*

1917

Wilhelmwerk, *Dralle Co.* (perfume and fine soaps)
Wilhelmwerk, *Continental Times* (German-American magazine)
Wilhelmwerk, *Shilsky Co.* (chemicals)

1917

Wilhelmwerk, *Hansa and Brandenbourg* (airplane manufacturer)

1917

Wilhelmwerk, *Siemens and Halske* (electric appliances)
Wilhelmwerk, *Heinrich Lanz Co.* (argricultural machinery)
Wilhelmwerk, *Paraguay Co.* (meat extract)
Wilhelmwerk, *Allgemeinen Elektrizitaets* (public electric company)

Wilhelmwerk, *A. Borsig* (machinery)

1917

Wilhelmwerk, *Otto Elsner Verlag* (publisher)

1917

Wilhelmwerk, *German Gymnastic Association*

1918

Maler Geyer, *L.W.Seidel and Sohn Inc.* (publisher and bookstore)
Maler Geyer, *Anton Schroll and Co.* (publisher?)

1918

Konrad Jochheim, *Lloyd's Cellufiber* (plastics)

1918

O. Baumberger, *Rascher and Co.* (publishers)
F.H.E., *"Die Propyläen"* (weekly magazine)

1918

Otto Hupp, *German Museum for Books and Script*

1919

Max Körner, *Württembourg Ev. Landeskirche* (mark for Protestant Church of Württembourg)

Max Körner, *Moser Roth* (automobiles?)

Konrad Jochheim, *Alfred Seher Co.* (mining equipment)

F.H.E., *Erhardt and Sehmer* (machine works)

1919

Max Körner, *Kickers* (type of company unknown)

1920

Max Körner, *Luftschiffbau Zepplin* (zepplins)
Unknown Artist, *J.F.Ziegler'sche* (book printer)

Max Körner, *Tapetenhous H.H.* (wallpaper)

1920

Unknown Artist, *Franz Richter* (publisher)
Max Schwerdtfeger, *Frankfurter Verlags Anstalt Inc.* (publisher)
Unknown Artist, *Franz Richter* (publisher)
F.H.E., *Gebr. Queck Nähnadelfabric* (needles)

1920

Hans Weiss, (unknown company)

1921

Unknown artist, *Erasmus Druck* (printer)

Prof. Hermann Virl, (unknown company)

1921

Wilhelm Degering, *Fa. Grathwohl* (type of Company unknown)
Wilhelmwerk, *Die Gebrueder Reuling* (type of company unknown)
Paul Renner, *Union of German Publishers*

1921

Traugott Schalcher, *"Vörwärts"* (publishing sign for Social Democrat political publishers)

1921

Max Körner, *Grossbuchbinderei Stuttgart* (book bindery)
Max Korner, *Pickenhahn Chemnitz* (type of company unknown)
Josef Mehlhard, (personal mark)
E. R. Bogenhauer, (personal mark for his printing company)

O.W. Hadank, *Arthur Collignon* (publisher)

1921

Hanns Thaddäus Hoyer, *M.W.Z. Zigarettenfabrik* (proposed design for cigarette company)

Ludwig Enders, *M.W.Z. Zigarettenfabrik* (cigarettes)

1921

Erich M. Etzold, *Ernst Reinhardt Co.* (publisher)
Heinrich Jost, *Tvorba Zagreber Fatzfabrik* (barrel maker)
Johann B. Maser, *A. Sedstein Co.* (art supplies?)
Erich M. Etzold, *Speditions Firma Heimerl* (forwarding-shipping)

1921

Konrad Jochheim, *Thüringer Mützenfabrik* (hats)

1921

Rudolph Koch, *Rudolfinischen Drucker Offenbach* (association of printing companies)
Rudolph Koch, *Werkstattgruppe* (arts workshops)

Heinrich Pauser, *Faber and Schleicher* (machinery)

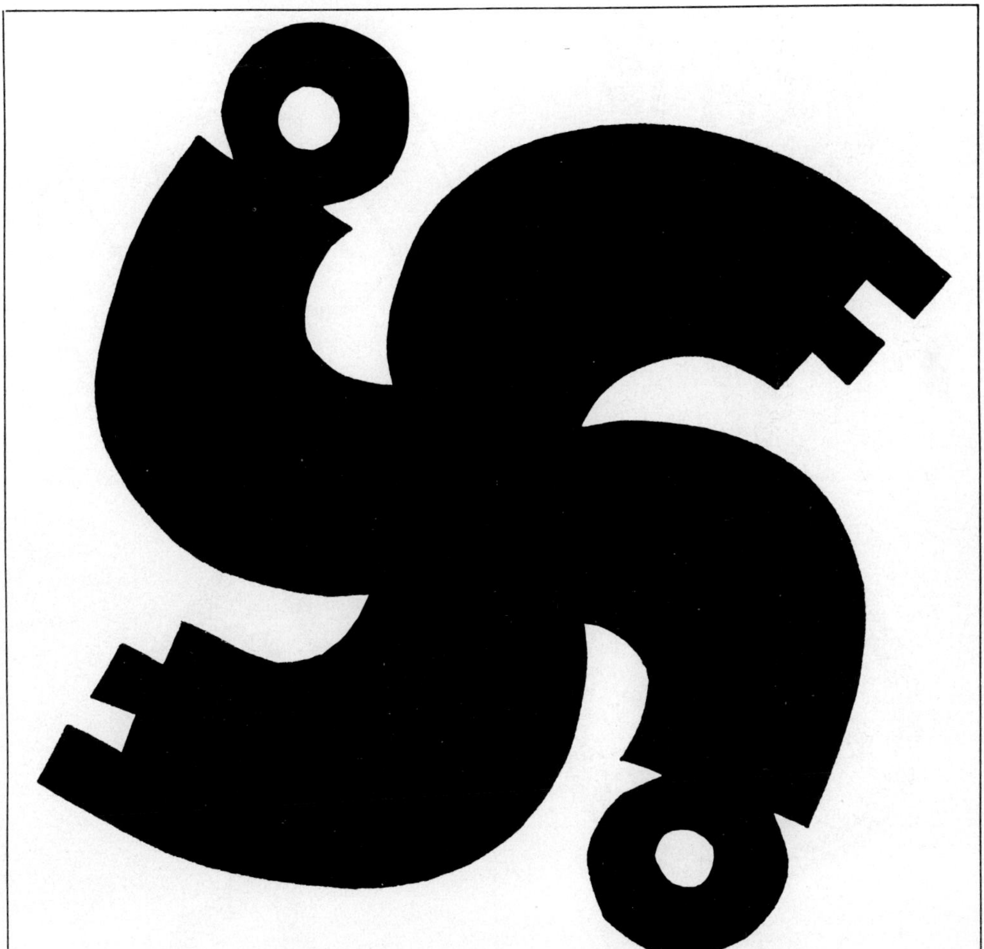

1921

Ernst Heigenmofer, (personal mark)
Prof. Emil Preetorius, *Roland Verlages* (publisher)
Heinrich Jost, *Hugo Bruckmann* (publisher)
Eduard Ege, *Josef Schaffner* (book bindery)

Hartmuth Pfeil, (insurance company)

1921

Ludwig Enders, *Philipps Söhne* (tobacco factory)

1921

Karl Schulpig, *Steinberg and Co.* (piano factory)

1921

Wilhelm Hensel, *Deutsche Graphik* (German Graphic)
Hermann Reimel, *A. Hartmann* (decorator?)
Edwin Henel, *Herdfabrik Wamsler* (stoves and boilers)
Heinrich Jost, *Drei Masten Verlages* (publisher)

Eduard Ege, *L. Pachtner Co.* (rubber factory-condoms)

1921

Konrad Jochheim, *Wender Co.* (auto dealer)
Paul Renner, *R. Piper and Co.* (publisher)
Hermann Lans, *Dr. Reinhold Horwath-Kraft* (personal mark)

1921

Konrad Jochheim, *Deutsche Werk* (household appliances)

1921

Karl Prinz, *Max Siefert, Direktor* (personal mark)
Georg Breitweiser, (chemical glaze company)

1921

Karl Schulpig, *Chemischen Fabrik Oberschöneweide* (chemical company)

1921

Albert Fuss, (rubbergoods company)

1921

Lucian Bernhard, *Grosseinkaufsgenossenschaft Abteilung Schneiderartikel* (association of wholesalers of tailor's supplies)

1921

Hans Thaddäus Hoyer, *Reinhold Dulce Co.* (printer)
Hans Bohm, *Frankfurter Verlags* (publisher)
Prof. J.V. Cissarz, *Flügel-Schmidt* (type of company unknown)
Hans Bohm, *Hauser Presse* (printer)

1921

Konrad Jochheim, *Rotations* (refridgerators and compressors)

1922

Prof. Hermann Virl, *Sankljohaunser, München* (type of company unknown)
Max Körner, (metal workshop)
Karl Schulpig, *Weigmann and Co.* (automobiles)
Max Körner, *Erhard and Sohne* (type of company unknown)

1922

Karl Schulpig, *Horbach and Schmitz* (wholesale steel)

1922

Prof. Hermann Virl, *Lebkuchenfabrik Doosa* (gingerbread baker)
Konrad Jochheim, *Vereinigte Industrieunternehumungen* (associated industrial enterprises)

1922

Karl Schulpig, *Krüger and Fahrenwaldt* (wholesale glass)

1922

Karl Schulpig, *A. and G. Schneider* (shoes)
F.H.E., *Otto Reichl Verlag* (publisher)
Max Körner, *Behringer and Co.* (type of company unknown)
Karl Schulpig, *Erich Blume Co.,* (hairnets)

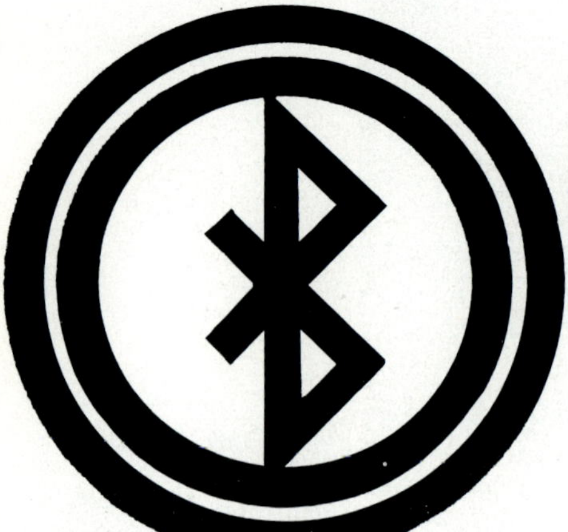

1922

Karl Schulpig, *Mette and Wrede* (meat jelly)

1922

Karl Schulpig, *Messeamt Köln am Rhein* (industrial exhibition in city of Köln)
Karl Schulpig, *C. Mugge Co.* (refreshing drinks)
Karl Schulpig, *L.W. Brandt and Co.* (exporters)

1922

Karl Schulpig, *Jak. Scherrer Co.* (Ladies' underwear)

1922

Karl Schulpig, *A. Herpich Söhne* (fur preservation)
Max Körner, *Wilhelm Renz Co.* (furniture factory)
Unknown artist, *Dieck and Co.* (publisher)

1922

Dieck and Company, various publishing signets

1922

F.H.E., *Wilhelm Stempfle Co.* (art publisher)
A. Paul Weber, *Oscar Brandstetter Co.* (publisher)
F.H.E., *Bayrische Textil-Werke* (fabric)

1922

Prof. Hermann Virl, (type of company unknown)

1922

Karl Schulpig, *J.S. Preuss* (workshop for books and printing)

PREUSS-DRUCK

1922

Karl Schulpig, *L.W. Brandt and Co.* (exporters)

1923

F.H.E., *Dr. Gerhard Niedermeyer* (personal marks)
F.H.E., *Rosenhammer* (type of company unknown)

1923

Konrad Jochheim, *Gustave Hamel and Co.,* (silk and cotton goods)

1923

Prof. Hermann Virl, *J. Rheimberger Co.* (printer and lithographer)

Karl Schulpig, *Addiator Inc.* (adding machines)

1923

Konrad Jochheim, *Runge and Kaulfuss* (fine mechanics and optics)
Karl Schulpig, *Richard Forster* (machinery)
Prof. Hermann Virl, (personal mark?)

1923

Konrad Jochheim, *Rosenberg Samenzucht und Samenhandlung* (seeds)

1923

Karl Schulpig, *Kraft Versicherungs* (insurance of auto clubs)

Karl Schulpig, *Allianz Versicherungs* (insurance)

ALLIANZ-KONZERN

1923

Karl Schulpig, *Phönix Kupferdruck* (copper printing)

1923

Karl Schulpig, *Goldmark Versicherungs Inc.* (insurance)

1923

Karl Schulpig, *C. Bolle Co.* (dairy)
Karl Schulpig, *G.A. Schreiber und Meinel* (musical instruments)
Karl Schulpig, *Ernst Kniepert Co.* (rubber works)
Karl Schulpig, *G.A. Schreiber und Meinel* (musical instruments)

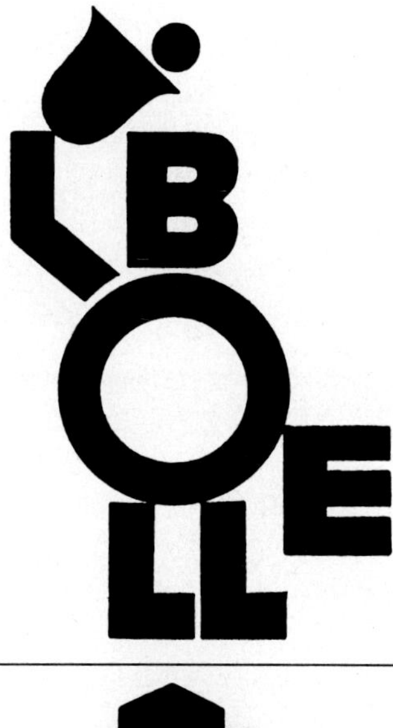

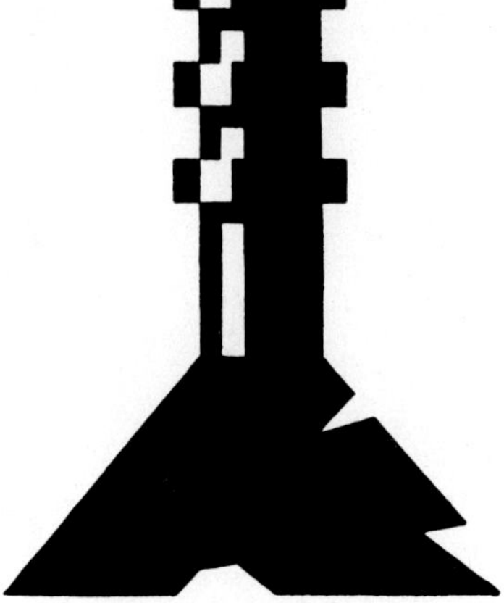

1923

Karl Schulpig, *Milchwerke Inc.* (dairy)

1923

Konrad Jochheim, *Orionette Co.* (motorcycles)
Lucian Zabel, *J. Rotschild* (type of company unknown)
Karl Bültmann, *Zigarettenfabrik Mewes, Wiesbaden* (cigarettes)

1923

Karl Schulpig, *Frerichswerft Inc.* (ship builders)

1923

Karl Schulpig, *Materna Kakao* (cocoa)

Karl Schulpig, *Heymann und Sohn* (kitchen appliances)

Karl Schulpig, *F.C. Glaser und R. Pflaum* (type of company unknown)

Karl Schulpig, *Rudolph and Co.* (chemical factory)

1923

Karl Schulpig, *Radium Gummiwerke* (rubber)

1923

Karl Schulpig, *Grosshaus Neuendorf* (department store)
Karl Schulpig, *Karl Saborsky Co.* (railroad parts)

QUANTO

1923

Karl Schulpig, *Dr. A. Schade* (personal mark for business man)

1923

Karl Schulpig, *Nord Deutsche Eisenbau* (North German iron works)
F.H.E., *R.F. Baudler und Co.* (reed furniture)
F.H.E., *Piper Drucke* (printer)
Karl Schulpig, *H. Leiser Co.* (shoes)

1924

Prof. Hermann Virl, *Albrecht Dürer* House

1924

Prof. Hermann Virl, *Schmidberger Co.* (printer)

1924

Prof. Peter Behrens, *R. Oldenbourg Co.* (printing and publishing)

1924

Walter Kersting, *M und B Verfügbarer* (type of company unknown)
Prof. Hermann Virl, *Werkstatt für feine Masschueiderei* (fine tailoring for women)
F.H.E., *Oskar Kayser Graphisches Verlag* (publisher)
Max Körner, *Millerwerke* (type of company unknown)

1924

F.H.E., *C.H. Beck'sche Verlagsbuchhandlung* (publisher's book store)

1924

Walter Kersting, *Elida Perfume* (two marks shown)
Max Korner, *Tabak-haus Philipp* (tobacco)
Max Körner, *Deutsche Wertarbeit* (type of company unknown)

1924

Hans Bergemann, *Agfa Farbenindustrie* (paints, photo supplies)

1924

Karl Schulpig, *Eduard Hubenthal Frankenhain* (type of company unknown)

L. Moholy-Nagy, *Kreis Der Freunde Des Bauhauses* (Circle Of Friends Of The Bauhaus)

1924

Karl Schulpig, *Der Bücherkreis* (reading room)
Karl Schulpig, *Deutsche Fensterglas* (window glass)

1924

F.H.E., *R.F. Baudler and Co.* (reed furniture)
Walter Kersting, *Tanne Co.* (type of company unknown)
F.H.E., *Zeitschrift Niedersachsen* (magazine for County of Niedersachsen)

1924

F.H.E., *Verlag Ullstein Inc.* (publisher)
F.H.E., *Gebr. Kaufmann Co.* (ladies clothing)
F.H.E., *Deutsche Verkehrs Ausstellung* (German Transportation Exhibition)

1924

Karl Schulpig, *Crescendo Verlag* (music publisher)

1924

F.H.E., *R. Piper and Co.* (publisher)
F.H.E., *Isidor Bach Inc.* (men's clothing)
Walter Kersting, *Molkerei Zentrale Oldenburg* (Dairy Center in Oldenburg)

1924

Karl Schulpig, *Wikinger Inc.* (type of company unknown)

1924

Karl Schulpig, *Teneriffa Co.* (cigarettes)
Karl Schulpig, *Wilhelm Eisenführ Co.* (type of company unknown)
Karl Schulpig, *Atlantic Zigarettenfabrik* (cigarettes)

EISENKOMET

1924

Unknown inhouse designer, *H. Sperling Co.* (book bindery)

1924

Karl Schulpig, *Woguna Co.* (chocolate)

1924

Karl Schulpig, *Heinrich Klein Co.* (coal)

1924

F.H.E., *Stern Und Unstern* (imprint of C.H. Beck'sche Publishing Co.)
Karl Schulpig, *Dera Rundfunk* (broadcasting)
Karl Schulpig, *Mensing Co.* (men's clothing)
F.H.E., *Fritz Tausky* (ladies' hats)

1924

Karl Schulpig, *Maga Margarinefabrik* (margarine)

MÄRKISCHE PERLE

1924

Karl Schulpig, *Meierei C. Bolle Inc.* (dairy)

Karl Schulpig, *Hans Hopp* (personal mark for engineer)

1924

Karl Schulpig, *Paul Eggebrecht Co.* (winery)
Max Körner, *Spielzeugausstellung Nürnberg* (Exhbition of Toys in Nurnberg)
Karl Schulpig, *Havenga Co.* (tobacco)

Otto Hupp, *"Books of the Middle Ages"*

1925

Prof. Hermann Virl, *Modegeschäft* (fasionable clothing shop)
A. Paul Weber, *Deutscher Drucker* (printer)
Prof. Hermann Virl, *Obstgrosshandlung Langemcier* (wholesale fruit)
Karl Schulpig, *Carl Brandt Inc.* (type of company unknown)

CARL BRANDT

1925

Konrad Jochheim, *Gebr. Heine Inc.* (mail order fabric)

1925

Karl Schulpig, *Vorm. Freiderich Bayer and Co.* (candy-bonbons)

1925

Karl Schulpig, *Agfa Co.* (photography)

1925

Max Körner, *Metalwaren Brand* (metal utensils)
Max Körner, *Wolf und Sohn* (type of company unknown)
Max Körner, *Zepplin Werke* (air ships-zepplins)

1925

Karl Schulpig, *Graubner Likörfabrik* (alcoholic beverage factory)

1925

Karl Schulpig, *Frankendruck Inc.* (printer)
Karl Schulpig, *Gustav Cords* (type of company unknown)
Karl Schulpig, *Dr. Arthur Salomonsohn* (personal mark?)
Karl Schulpig, *Gardinefabrik Paul Becker* (curtain factory)

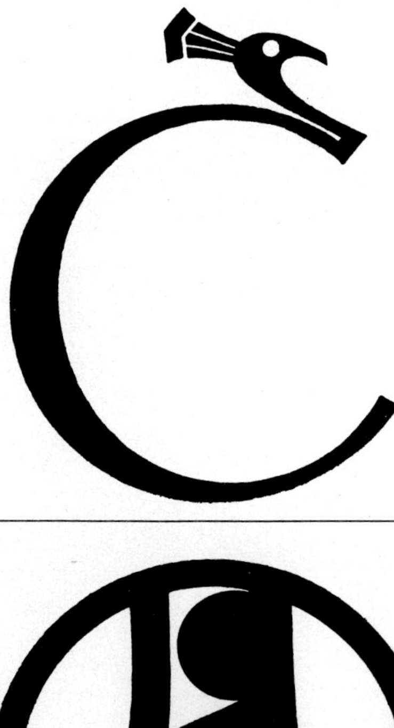

1925

Karl Schulpig, *Friedrich Goerig Co.* (metal hardening agents)

1925

Karl Schulpig, *W. Vogt Jr. Geschaftbucher* (account books)

Johannes Boehland, *Verlag Deutscher Wille* (publisher)

Leon Amar, *Berek Druck* (advertising agency and printer)

Karl Schulpig, *Deutscher Sparkassen Und Giroverband* (savings bank and clearing house)

1925

Karl Schulpig, *Bernhard Kass Inc.* (children's clothing?)

1925

Karl Schulpig, *Werhahnmüle Neuss* (mill)

Lucian Zabel, *Eichhorn Apotheke* (pharmacy)

EICHHORN
APOTHEKE

Leslie James Cabarga is an illustrator and designer in New York City. His clients include Time magazine, The New York Times, Rolling Stone, The National Lampoon, CBS Records, Atlantic Records, and all of the major advertising agencies. He creates hand lettering and trademark designs for clients under the nom de plume, "Lettering By Handy". This is his second book on an esoteric subject the first having been "The Fleischer Story" (Nostalgia Press, 1976) about the pioneering film animators, the Fleischer Brothers, creators of many memorable cartoons and advances in the technique of film animation.

Steve Heller is art director of the New York Times Book Review. He has produced exhibits of German and French art including "The Art of Simplicissmus". His latest book is "Man Bites Man — Two Decades of Satiric Art" (A. and W. Publishers, 1981).

margo
chase
design
2255
bancroft
ave
los angeles
california
90039
213
668 1055